The bag of coal

Written by Wes Magee

Illustrated by Val Biro

Heinemann

Nesta and Ned were little dragons.
One day they went to play
in the sky.

'I can see Grandma Dragon,'
said Nesta.
'Why is she so sad?'

3

Nesta and Ned flew down
to see Grandma.

'Why are you so sad, Grandma?'
said Nesta.
'That Big Bad Dragon flew off with
my bag of coal,' said Grandma.
'Now I have no coal to eat.'

'We will find your bag of coal,'
said Ned.
So Nesta and Ned flew up
into the sky.

Nesta and Ned looked for
Big Bad Dragon.
Then Nesta saw him in Wild Wood.
'There he is,' she said.

Nesta and Ned flew down to Wild Woo
Big Bad Dragon had the bag of coal.
They saw him eat the coal.

'We can make him go,' said Nesta.
'WHOOO!' called the dragons.
'WHOOOOOOOO!'

Big Bad Dragon jumped up.
'G-g-g-g-ghosts!' he said.
'I d-d-d-don't like g-g-g-ghosts!'
Big Bad Dragon ran and ran.

Big Bad Dragon ran into the pond.

'Come on Ned,' called Nesta.

'Now we can get the bag of coal.'

Nesta and Ned flew to Grandma
with the coal.
'Now you can eat your coal,' said Ned.
Grandma was very happy.